The Poetic Collection Of
A Traveler's Experiences In Israel

LIONFISH

Brad Jacobson

Mazo Publishers

Lionfish
Copyright © 2020 Brad Jacobson

ISBN 978-1-946124-64-7

Contact The Author
bradjacobsonp@gmail.com

Mazo Publishers
Website: www.mazopublishers.com
Email: mazopublishers@gmail.com

Dedicated to

Priya Jacobson
My wife and soul mate

Pamela Lazarus
Volunteer Coordinator of Sar-El

CONTENTS

Part Two

THE AUTHOR

Brad Jacobson grew up in Wilmington, DE. Although he was not serious about Israel or his Jewish faith, that all changed when his mother bought him an airplane ticket  to Israel and he became a volunteer on Kibbutz Maabarot. Since that first summer experience, he has returned to Israel more than 30 times to be both a volunteer and traveler.

Brad has an MED in Literacy from the University of Missouri (MU) and an MS in Recreation from Southern Illinois University. He has taught English as a second language at the Asian Affairs Center at MU.

Brad has also worked with students with disabilities in sports and recreation. He is an avid exerciser. In Israel, he enjoys hiking and scuba diving.

PART ONE

ROCKS AND STARS

I asked the Rocks how many Stars.
I asked the Stars how many Rocks.
I didn't get an answer –

So I asked the Camel –

The Camel just laughed.

So I started to count
The Rocks in the Sky
And the Stars on the Ground

CHUTZPAH

Everyone claps.
Everyone knows the words.

Riding Bus 38 from the Old City,
a crowd mingling by the outdoor theater.
Shlomo Artzi is playing here tonight.

Sold out. Two people go in
under the rope and I follow them.

I have Shlomo Artzi's CDs in America,
but here I watch him
jump up and down on stage.

Everyone claps.
Everyone knows the words.

I tell Ester about it the next day.
She tells me I am getting chutzpah,
she tells me I am becoming Israeli.

LIONFISH TELL ME

You look like a Picasso,
Eighteen paper wings in flight.

They say you have a poison dagger,
but I am not afraid of you, old Lionfish.

Your face has an old sadness like a father
who watched his child become a soldier.

Lionfish, did you use your dagger to kill
the Pharaoh's soldiers?

Is that why we say Red Sea?

Lionfish says,
"No, I saw a mother steal
a pomegranate for her crying child."

YAACOV

Tekia-Tekia.
Blasts of the shofar horn,

Out the window,
Mt. Meron is painted
against the purple
and rose sky,
talking to the stars.

Tekia-Tekia.

I sound out
the Hebrew letters
in the prayer book
bet-resh-vav-chaf – pronouncing *"ba-r-u-ch"*.
It is Rosh Hashanah,
the new year – 5778.

I gaze up.
The entire congregation
stands. I quickly rise.

The man next to me does the same.
His name is Yaacov,
a rabbi I met yesterday.

Yaacov tells me
he's been going
to services for thirty-three years,
still gets it wrong.

I understand.
He did not want me
to stand alone.

FALLING STAR

A camel's grunt, Awad's Bedouin tea.
He scrambles up rocks like a mountain goat
in flimsy sandals.

In leather hiking boots,
I tumble down like a falling star.

Hiding in the shade of a rock
I drink sweet tea
by thirsty mountains,
then swim in a desert pond with water bugs.

Bedouins say,
"Hamza ally, Hamza wadi" – high five, low five.

We see a Menorah and five slim goat figures
carved in rock.

Under a black tarp two men play backgammon
with game pieces from camel dung.

A flock of men in long white gowns
rise up then bow down
to pray.

The silence is like
the black holes between the stars.

The goat's neck is slit.
Then another.
For a wedding feast.

I sit beside the evening campfire
joining the Bedouins and camels.

Night signals from so many stars.

Climbing Mt. Sinai to see sunrise.
Beside a smooth sidewalk, a sharp gathering of rocks.
My path is too easy, just walking on the moon.

In a knick-knack shop
a well-dressed man
from Iowa
asks me
about my Phillies cap.

Out of place,
I am wearing a dirty t-shirt
and ragged shorts,

He's a shiny-shoed tourist
in a cushy bus,

different species.

In St. Katherine's monastery,
a dim-lit room like a cave.

Monk skulls in the middle
and bones on the side.

Eye sockets stare at me.

I turn around
to look at the flesh on people's cheeks.

SIVAN, ALONE

Seven times, she circles
her hands over the candle flames.

Dreams of a camel ride in the Negev.

Finishes work by noon every Friday.
Buys salmon and challah at the shuk.

Sings like an Old World Oriole
To welcome the Shabbat Queen.

Wax drips mirror her tears.

She cooks the fish with cut-up potatoes,
rosemary, paprika, and black pepper.

Sits next to her grandmother's empty wooden chair.
Says the Kiddush and drinks a cup of wine.

Does not touch the light switch.
Follows Shabbat with her whole heart,

All pure faith.
She feels a small piece of heaven.

COME IN, COME IN

Walking by the Kotel
Rabbi Machlis calls out
to Kenyan and Chinese tourists,
"Shabbat Shalom, Shabbat Shalom!"

Yesterday two soldiers
were stabbed in the Arab shuk.
I ask the rabbi if he is concerned –
He says, "No, I am with you."

We meet a Muslim beggar.
The rabbi invites him along.
At his home, people gather.
I squeeze into a corner seat.

Rabbi Machlis booms:
"Come in, come in,
there is plenty of room."
The homeless man, tourist,
soldier, Christian, Muslim, and Jew
eat cholent, challah, and gefilte fish.

"Each one of you is our special guest.
Almost each time I come back home
there are tears in my eyes," he says.

"We are in Jerusalem."

Rabbi Machlis calls me the scuba diver
– he knows I love to dive in the Red Sea –
and asks me to speak next.

I talk about my dive yesterday
and the Stingray.

We are in Jerusalem.

LITTLE YELLOW STAR

Yad Vashem – Holocaust Museum

A candle reflected in the mirror:
  One thousand candles reflected back.

One thousand smiling faces:
  Three, four, ten years old.

Open my eyes:
  The sky shines with little lights.

Close my eyes.
  The sky is full of desert stars.

THE FISHERMAN AND ME

I walked out on the pier
by an old man fishing, in a rickety boat.
I sat on a small white plastic bucket, next to his boat
I took out my camera,
placed it between my legs.
The old fisherman yelled,
"*Lech Me Po, Lech Me Po*" (Leave Me Alone, Leave Me Alone).

I kept sitting,
then pointed my camera again.
He took out a garden hose
and squirted me good.
I stood up and walked away.

Next day I walked out
on that same pier
and sat on that bucket.
I lifted the camera
to make peace
and put it into my bag.

The fisherman started talking,
invited me to come on his boat.
Said his name is Rahid – just like the city in Saudi Arabia.
He asked me to have coffee.
Rahid said there were 99 names
for G-d but just one G-d.

He said he is a Muslim.
I said I am a Jew.

The old fisherman and me
sat on his boat together.

I hate coffee,
but I drank it anyway.

MY NAME IS GVANTSA

Opah calls me Tiny.
When I was six years old
my grandfather took me
to shoot clay ducks.
They broke into a thousand
little stones.
In my army test, I had
twenty shots.
Each bullet hit the bullseye.

With a heavy backpack,
I had to march and run 50 kilometers.
I am not strong
but told myself not to quit.
My commander was so proud,
he gave me his red cap.

Red boots
mean I am a fighting soldier –
a sniper in the Israeli army.

Guarding the border,
a six-year-old boy from Sudan
waved a gun at me.
I thought of my baby sister – Eti.
She is my Tiny. I just stood there.
A covered woman walked towards me.
Her stomach was very big.
I knew it
wasn't a baby
and shot her in the leg.

At home I am just a girl.
I love to dance.

NARROW BRIDGE

A young Palestinian woman wearing a headscarf comes to class late.

She lost her cousin in a traffic accident.

Our teacher, a Jewish mother, hugs and kisses her on the cheek.

Later, the teacher whispers a secret to a student in front, who whispers to a student next to them. The secret goes around the class to students from fourteen countries:

Austria, Holland, Brazil, South Korea, Germany.

The secret is

We study Hebrew at Beit Ha'am.

Our teacher plays the guitar and sings:

The world is a narrow bridge.

BEGGAR WOMAN

Lavanna
reaches out and sings,
"Help a sick, sick old woman."
Points to her heart and a shofar horn rings.
Twirls red string around a clump of thread the mass
and shape of a lopsided cheese knish.

Once a young girl with red curls, sly
and sixteen. Worked in a fancy dress shop
and stole two men's hearts.
She sings, "A few lucky gems by
the Wailing Wall in Jerusalem."
Twirls her red string.

Every day I sling two shiny
shekel coins into her eloquent hands.
She cries, "Mister, Mister,
a sick, sick old woman."
Points to her heart and a shofar horn rings.
Twirls her red string.

I ask, "Have you seen Ester—the shopkeeper?"
She says, "She is like my sister."
"Have you seen Rabbi Aaron?"
She snorts, "Oh, you mean Gingi.
He teaches gossip is like feathers
blowing in the wind. You can never
take them back.

I gaze into her green eyes
and say, "Beautiful, beautiful."
The beggar woman winks and blows me a kiss.
Asks my mother's name and says a prayer.
Wraps a red string around my wrist and sings
of my mother's stuffed cabbage, kugel, and borsch.

RED SEA DIVE

Exhale, inhale
The same rhythm as praying
at the Wailing Wall

A giant sea turtle
swims lazily over
Joshua's Rock

Bubbles rise
like songs
of Shabbat

The sun drops
over the Red Sea mountains
like the blue and white

Havdalah candle
dipping into
Mogen David Wine

THE RABBI

In the courtyard of the Wailing Wall, a black-bearded man in a black suit asks where I am from and if I am Jewish.

I think, "What it is to you?" but I tell him, "I am from America and I am Jewish."

He asks what am I doing in Israel."

I am working on a kibbutz," I say.

He asks me, "What can you learn about being Jewish digging dirt?" I look at him.

"Come to a Shabbat dinner," he says and points to a large circle of people standing by the water fountains. "They are all going to be guests tonight."

I say, "I am going to meet my kibbutz friends soon."

He tells me it is better to go for a Shabbat meal and we duel back and forth. Eventually, he wins. He introduces himself as Rabbi Schuster and tells me to stand here and he will come back for me.

I wait. I watch the large crowd gathered at the wall. I watch the soldiers dancing with men dressed in black. Finally, the crowd starts to disperse and the circle of people gathered by the water fountain gets much smaller.

Here comes the rabbi to get me. We walk a short way to the stairs, up many steps and down the alley. We stop and the rabbi knocks on a front door. A man in white invites me in and the rabbi quickly leaves. Well-dressed guests are gathered in a handsome apartment. I am wearing a t-shirt, shorts, and running shoes. I take a deep breath.

Guests sit down. I am shown a place to sit by three young men in suits. They are talking. Their accent is British. The men sing a few songs. Guests rise. I follow one of the Brits to the kitchen sink. The young man hands me a special cup and explains what to do.

I pour water three times on my right hand and then three times on my left hand. He helps me with a prayer. I go back to the table and everyone is silent. There is something special in the silence. The man cuts a very large loaf of bread and starts passing a plate full of it around the table. I take a piece. We each have a cup of wine. Soon the table is noisy, full of conversation and home-cooked food. It is much better than the kibbutz dining hall.

The man starts to tell a story.

Shabbat, he begins, is the time for ourselves. All week we work, we are in a hurry. But on Shabbat we take the time to be free. It is not the time to watch television, we don't work or do our school lessons. We have time to spend with our family and friends. We have good food; we have time to reflect.

We are free to be ourselves.

Every seven days we are given one day to rest and enjoy.

SOUP KITCHEN

Shabbat candles
Red Wine
Splash water on my right hand
and then left hand

Silence

Nosh of Challah
Wailing Wall in view

Matzo Ball Soup
Hummus
Tomatoes and cucumbers
Chicken

Sit across from a young man
He has a kind face

Angels join us

A PRAYER

Yesterday
I have jogged here a hundred times
along the beach in Jaffa
But not since last September

A new monument stands close by
Photographs of 22 victims
Suicide bomber at a dance club

A woman throws a stick into the water
Her dog fetches

People play paddleball
as if nothing happened

Rocks touch the gentle sea

I stand by the monument
See young faces and life

There are no words
I pray

Today
Standing in the post line in Jaffa
A woman in front of me could be a college student
wearing the traditional abaya
In front of her, a Muslim woman talks casually
with a Jewish woman

The Arab woman wears a headscarf
The Jewish woman wears jeans

I think to myself
They should be our leaders

LION OF HOPE

Black stocking feet and no shoes.
Blue and white prayer shawl
wrapped around his head and arms.

He stands in front of the ancient Wall,
his face hidden.

Large as a lion, he raises his hands
like a street performer before the worshipers.

He sweeps his arms above the old man in white,
above a boy in a blue baseball jersey, #32,
above the rabbi in back of the Torah.

The Lion of Hope roars,
and his prayers
speed like Lefty's fastball,
soar to the top of Mt. Moriah,
pure as tears protecting a child's prayer.

He steps slowly to a chair by mine.
I touch the Wall and hear
the Big Man whispers,
"I am exhausted."

After prayers we walk together
to the Kiddush table by the stairs.

The Rabbi raises a cup of wine.
Big Man turns to sing sweet
Shabbat songs to Chinese tourists.

He shakes my hand.

"Shabbat Shalom. Be healthy. Have peace."

ELENA

My parents were teachers in a deaf school in Jordan.
Our neighbors brought us sweets.

I am the little girl with blond hair and blue eyes.
The neighbors pinched my cheeks.

To be Jewish, the rabbi said we should live by Jews.
Now there is a fence instead of treats.

This time it was a mother on the road to Jerusalem.
We stand silently on aching feet.

NO BORDERS (I)

Moonbeams ballet over the desert mountains of Jordan across the Red Sea.

I fall asleep to quiet splashes and nomadic stars.

I wake and watch an early morning swimmer as the sun rises over the mountains, lighting up Mother Earth.

In the West, the half-round moon bows down over the desert mountains of Israel.

Moon, sun, stars, sea, mountain, desert – Hashem is everywhere.

DREAMING OF PEACE, TAKING NOTES (I)

My shorts torn, I search for a tailor shop.

Turning right, I walk past the citadel, to the parking lot of the four synagogues. By Ramban's Synagogue, a boy holds a kippah on his head while chasing a soccer ball.

In the open square, Japanese tourists take photographs of the Hebrew Alef-Bet artwork by the Jewish Quarter artist, Esther Weiss.

Over there, behind the ancient olive press, an Arab baker sells kosher bagels from an old green cart.

The sweet fragrance reminds me of Aunt Nitza's cheese blintzes. I reach the Kotel. One hundred men dressed in black daven in a Hasidic choir to Go-d.

A worshiper wearing a Phillies cap folds a crying note carefully into a narrow crevice between 2000-year-old stones and turns to smile for family pictures.

I walk through a stone tunnel.
Yesterday a rock thrower wounded my friend near here.
A teenage soldier keeps guard. I shut my eyes.

An Arab boy passes me, pushing a heavy cart of Kunafa shredded orange dough with saffron from Ja'far Sweets. Two shopkeepers play shesh-besh outside their shops. One of them calls out to me, "Look in my bazaar: Bedouin rugs, menorahs, jewelry – a gift?"

A Muslim man slips off his shoes in front of an eight-hundred-year-old white stone wall to pray on an embroidered rug pointing towards Mecca. A woman wearing a white-fringed head scarf and a long black abaya sits on a wooden stool selling grape leaves. She reaches out to me and pleads... shesh shekels. I stop by Michael's stand and order pita with hummus, salad, and falafel.

Next door is a sewing shop, so I go in. I sit by the tailor and watch him sew my shorts. He is an Arab, I am a Jew, waiting in my underwear.

SHABBAT SHALOM

Slouched, ash smudged
cheeks, patched black
pants and coat, he lugs
three white sacks uphill.

Perfect photo, I imagine,
but blurt out, "Can I help?"

He pauses,
then grins and gazes up
at the early morning sky,
as if he's looking at Hashem.

He greets me,
"Shabbat Shalom,"
and keeps walking.

SHABTAY, MADRICH

Shabtay picks me up at the Greenhouse Hostel on the way to his home. I attack the schnitzel, salad, and chocolate cake Rooty has prepared for me. Afterwards Shabtay gives me a ride to the bus to meet the other volunteers.

Tonight we are going back to the archeological dig. Twenty years and Shabtay has never stopped being my madrich. Every morning on the army base we hear a knock on the door and Shabtay calling: *Boker tov, Boker tov,* Good Morning, Good Morning.

On my wedding day he gave Priya a tour of the city and serenaded us, singing with a band at the Artist Market. Shabtay has given me pieces of memories, pieces of Israel.

Here a British soldier commanded his father to stop.
If he obeyed he would be sent to jail or released
by Arab gangs in Jaffa that would attack him.
So he ran and was shot in the shoulder and leg.
He swam a half kilometer in the Mediterranean
to the beach in Tel Aviv. February, 1948.

Shabtay saw people dancing and celebrating
in the streets. Families listened to the radio.
Israel was declared a free nation by the United Nations.
War was the next day. He was 9. May, 1948.

Shabtay was a principal of a high school in Jaffa.
"My students were beautiful and intelligent,"
he told me. Tension was in the air, remnunts
of yesterday's attack. The Arab students had the option
to stay at school but chose to go with the Jewish students
to celebrate Holocaust Memorial Day. April, 2003.

Shabtay is training for a distance swim in the Kineret.
He picks me up at B'nai Dan and we go to his pool
to swim laps. Shabtay says he returns to his school
once a year on Memorial Day to honor his students
that fell in the wars. June, 2018.

YOM KIPPUR

Before
sunset
I snack
on dates,
almonds,
and potato
burekas.

A little boy
with paos
scoots
by me
on his tricycle
in the middle
of the road.

Near the
synagogue
people,
not cars,
are parked.

No one puts
shekels into
parking meters.

On King George Street
people sit
in a circle
singing.

Isaac
glances
at the
rear view
mirror.

He prays
and meditates.

This
started
before
the earth
was born.

SIX CAMELS

Church bells and Arab prayers
moan out of the loudspeaker.
The bus driver's foot presses the pedal to the floor.
Old City Wall and David's Citadel fade from view.
We enter a tunnel and begin descending.

A plywood Bedouin shack and a white pickup truck.
I wonder if the TV antenna gets cartoons from Jordan.
A teenage girl in a black burka clutches a broken stick
herds twenty goats across the dusty road.
Six camels pose by the mountains.

The Masada plateau.
I imagine voices of Jewish zealots.
The Romans took three years to build
a siege ramp to the top
and tomorrow they will enter. The zealots choose ten men
and then one
until all 960 voices vanish.

At a rest stop,
I ease my toes into the Dead Sea.

*Dedicated to the memory of my friend Jim Baden, a great
teacher and storyteller.*

AT SAMMY'S STORE

Today is Shabbat.
I stop in for a Bamba
Peanut snack and coke.

We do not pay
until after Shabbat.
Sammy wears a Yankees hat.

His first language is Arabic
but he speaks English and Hebrew
to customers.

David visits Sammy every day.
He manages the Heritage House,
the Jewish hostel next door.

Sammy, David and I dream about sailing
around the world together. We will meet
at the ship tomorrow or the day after.

OASIS

"Come – come into my store," the shopkeeper calls.

Walking through the Arab shuk, I focus straight ahead.

"A special deal for you," he says.

I eye a Bedouin carpet hanging outside his store.

The shopkeeper invites me to sit and have coffee
and tells me his name is Neal.

I am his first customer in twelve days.

He says both Palestinians and Jews have hearts ... and that
he loves to eat hummus and drink Coke with my friends.

I pick out a candle holder, but can't find my wallet.
I am his first customer in twelve days.

He looks under the pillow.
Finds the black billfold and teases me,
"Where is my wallet – where is my wallet?"

We laugh together.

TWENTY-ONE PHOTOGRAPHS

Sari invites me to go up north with her for the day. She is a tour guide and is scouting out next week's trip. She picks me up at the Greenhouse, my hostel in Tel Aviv. In the car is Maiya. She has red hair and freckles and is a student at Hebrew University. During the drive Maiya tells me that she played the rabbit in Alice in Wonderland. Then she tells me a story.

This past January her parents were in France on vacation. It was just Maiya and her younger brother at home. Her brother was a medic in the army. One morning Maiya woke up to news on the radio that there was a suicide bombing at the bus junction near their home. Her brother waited at this bus stop every morning. Maiya attempted to call her brother several times. She waited at home for his phone call. At 11 am the call came. He helped with the injured.

On our drive back we stop at this same junction – the Beit Lid. There are photographs of the twenty-one victims. Almost all were soldiers between the ages of 18-21.

I heard the news of this tragedy in Missouri. It was the same junction that was by my Kibbutz. I had been there many times. I felt alone in Missouri.

It is July, six months later, and I stand with Sari and Maiya in front of the 21 photographs.

TRUE STORY

A bird circles
Black and grey
Sounds a crow caw

Waits and circles
For Gill every morning
He brings crumbs from the shekum

The bird flies down
Snatches the food Gill leaves
Sometimes takes bread from his hands

The bird skirts away
Later steals a sandwich
When a woman isn't watching

A bird circles
Waits for Gill
Sounds a crow caw

BUS 405

I am on Bus 405 going from Jerusalem to Tel Aviv. Sitting next to me is a Canadian woman. She tells me that last night, she watched the opening of the Maccabiah Games on TV. The camera showed a Lithuanian athlete trying to sing the Israeli National Anthem but he didn't know all the words. When he saw the camera pointed at him, he smiled. She says that it was so beautiful that she had tears in her eyes.

When we get off the bus, we hear the news.

While riding to Tel Aviv, another Bus 405 going back to Jerusalem was driven off a cliff.

UNDERSTAND ME

Crossing the road, I see four phone cords dangling down from their hooks. Rabbi Seidel, whom we met at the Wall, told us to wait on the corner by the phones. Three of us are invited for Shabbat dinner in Mea Shearim, an ultra-orthodox neighborhood.

An older Hasidic man greets us and introduces himself as Rabbi Weiss. I tell him my name is Brad. He asks me my last name and where my family is originally from. I tell him, "Jacobson" and that my grandparents were from Russia and Latvia. He tells me that in Israel, people pronounce the "J" as "Y," so it is pronounced "Yacobson."

He leads us up a narrow street. Bearded men with black suits and fur hats and women with covered hair stroll past. No cars or buses on the roads at the beginning of Shabbat. It could be Poland two hundred years ago.

When we arrive at his house, it is full of family and guests. We sit at the table, men on one side and women on the other.

Rabbi Weiss says he came to this neighborhood from Romania in 1950. He asks many questions: What am I doing in Israel? What are my plans? What do I do in America? He talks gently trying to forge a connection.

He makes a comment that will glue itself inside of me.

He says, "I do not know what you know but you do not know what I know."

A HASIDIC JEW AND SCUBA DIVER

In Jerusalem,
a Hasidic Jew dances at the Kotel to welcome Shabbat.

In the Red Sea, a scuba diver searches for Moses' Rock.

Avi's wife and daughter light the Shabbat candles.

I check my regulator (120 cc of air)
and keep heading toward the caves.

Avi raises the Kiddush cup and recites a prayer.

An octopus camouflaged by the coral
barely lifts its head.

Avi dips the blue and white candle
into King David's Wine.

I follow the last bubble to the surface.

We meet at a bagel shop.
Avi orders a tuna bagel. I get matzo ball soup.

PART TWO

BASEBALL

October 29, 2018

Dear Hadas,

What happened in the Tree of Life Synagogue
is beyond words.

There was a vigil at Peace Park in Columbia.
I saw two peace activists that are supporters
of the Palestinians.

Like you, I grew up as an invisible Jew.

My childhood friends were Christian.
We played baseball in the school yard.

Kids yelled, "Dirty Jew."
I kept quiet.

Santa filled my Christmas stocking with toys.
On Chanukah we lit candles but it wasn't nearly as fun.

After my college graduation my mother gave me
a gift – an airplane ticket to Israel.

I was blindsided. I loved being a volunteer
on Kibbutz Maabarot and traveling
to Jerusalem and Sinai.

When I came back to Delaware
my heart was still in Israel.

For the first time, I was proud to be Jewish.

Shalom,
Brad

DREAMING OF PEACE, TAKING NOTES (II)

A band of children crowd Sari and me
by Lion's Gate in the Old City of Jerusalem.

They sell postcards.

I hear,
"A postcard for a shekel.
How about a group of five?"

Children press into me.

A Palestinian man approaches.
Hands me my wallet and asks if everything is there inside.

I look and nod my head yes.

He tells me,
"We are not all bad,"

and walks away.

BAR MITZVAH

An easy swing.
Get a hit, I tell myself.
Four for four and one last at bat.

The bat meets the ball
and sails over the left field fence.

I didn't go to Hebrew school.

A trot around the bases –
an all-star on the Gwyn Hurst Blue Jays.

After graduating from college,
my mom asks if I want to go to Israel.
She knows my dream is to travel
to Thailand, Iceland, or anywhere.

My bar mitzvah is at the Wailing Wall.
I focus on each letter of the Hebrew prayer.
Like watching red stitches on a curveball.

It's an easy swing and trot around the bases.
High fives at home plate
with Rabbi Dyan, Avi, and Moishe.
 We celebrate at a bagel shop.

The next day my friend says he saw me on TV.

Mom cheers from the upper deck in the sky.

BOXES OF FOOD

Today we go to another base.

Work with eighty female soldiers
training to be medics.

Our job is to fill boxes of food.
We work until almost midnight.

Fill 11,880 boxes.
Each provides four meals.

My job is putting in cans of tuna.
Julie, a soldier, keeps the boxes close to me
so I can fill them quickly.

The soldiers start singing,
"She Justs Wants to Dance."

A volunteer says this is one
of the best days in her life.

Me too.

JAMBOREE

Seek the sacred within the ordinary
   – Rabbi Nachman of Breslov

Another sizzling day.
Suddenly, dark clouds.

Raindrops, pouring rain.
"Rain in June is crazy,"
I tell my boss.

"Rain today is special.
There were not the usual winter storms.
Now it hardly rains until after Sukkot,"
Amnon says.

On my early morning walk I stroll by two green
wheelbarrows with purple, red, and white flowers.

Suddenly, dark clouds. The cook drives by.
He always waves but today offers me a ride.
Raindrops. Pouring rain.

Rap Red, Lighting, Purple Jazz, Thunder and Drums, Indigo

Jamboree in the Sky

UPSTAIRS / DOWNSTAIRS, 1947

She washes gunpowder off her shoes.
As the washing machine rotates,
she ascends a spiral staircase
that disappears to the bakery.

On the first floor, British soldiers sip tea and eat cake.
She works eleven hours in dim light making bullets.
To tan, she spends time under blue lights.
She needs to look like a kibbutznik.

So many, just out of their teens, work in the basement.
They live in a fake kibbutz by a British military camp.
Outside are chicken coops and a tractor.
The chimney mixes the smell of gunpowder
with the sugar of sweets.

Washing machines above
block the noise.
The workers make three thousand bullets a week
and smuggle them out in milk jars.
The washing machine rotates.

She looks like an American college student,
shorts and t-shirt, a smooth-skinned co-ed.
A soldier sips spice tea.
She walks past him.

ROOF TOP IN THE OLD CITY

In a sleeping bag on a rooftop
in the Old City I can reach the stars.

The sunrise splatters in the middle
of the mosque and the synagogue.

Tuvia with the red curls and a white gown
strums Amazing by Bruno Mars
on King David's bronze harp
sitting atop the Church of Seventy Languages.

At the Wailing Wall, bearded men
in black suits bob up and down.

Avoda bows ten times.
Each time he picks up a cigarette butt.

A wrinkled angel crumbles a prayer,
maybe a joke, into crying rocks.

Stones smell like 2000-year-old books.

Garbage cans clank-clank at sunrise.
Hadas feeds a line of twenty cats
below the bullet holes at Zion's gate.

Esther wanders with Rachel
over ancient alleyways.

I fall asleep to the old lullabies.

SPLASH

Long blond dreadlocks greet
me. "The water is your friend,"
Guy says.

Hot and sweaty,
arriving from Jerusalem on
the bus,
I dive into the sea.

A tiny upwards gasp
on the coral.
An octopus scurries along.
A bluegrass band –
Little Goldfish, Big Blue,
Porcupine and Picasso.

We play Tonto
and chase the Lone Ranger –
Ten meters down.

A tiny Lizard fish disappears
into the sand.
Tal signals everything is ok.

Prehistoric head,
craggy body,
camouflaged by brother rocks,
growling at me,
Sagit waves her fingers no.

Later she tells me
the Stonefish is poisonous.

Dive 30 meters down
to the Satille – a sunken
ship.

Kick inside the open cabin
and Eran does a somersault.
Points at me to follow.

Back in the office,
Amit tells me,

*"I am going to put you on a
hook and leave you for the
octopus."*

I think of her laugh now,
and I miss her.

SUNRISE AT WAILING WALL

A man with a black hat and beard asks,
"Did you put on tefillin today?"
How about doing a mitzvah?"

"Ok," I reply and he unzips
an old blue bag, takes out
two black boxes and leather straps.

He reads a prayer in Hebrew
pauses to let me follow.

He places a black box
around my bicep, pointing
at my heart and wraps a black leather strap
seven times around my forearm,
the number of colors in a rainbow.

He stands on his tip-toes
and lifts my Phillies cap
to place a black box on my forehead.
It points towards heaven. He puts
my baseball cap back. Maybe now
the Phillies will win the pennant.

He instructs me to read the Shema.
Six holy words.

I close my eyes and recite
the prayer by heart.

I recall the story of soldiers who were ambushed
during the Six Day War. The enemy ran away
when they saw them wearing tefillin.

They thought the black boxes were bombs.

CAN OF BEANS

Little Gilad[1] wrote a story about a fish and a shark
who became friends
Is this a prophecy or a question mark?

Gilad's mother knits by her son's empty chair
Yesterday Aviva and Noam shared Gilad's birthday cake
from the Ben Yehuda street fair

Maiyan stays in front of the Minister's house,
a soldier in 1948
She guards the flowers and prayer books,
waiting for Gilad to celebrate

Tuval sleeps in the Sukkah and for lunch has a can of beans
She hands out yellow ribbons
Has long brown hair and is only fourteen

A girl sits on her father's shoulders and sings
to have her brother back
25,000 demonstrators march to have their brother back
A SAR-EL volunteer tells a story about Gilad erased in black

Gilad makes a wish that the fish is free from the shark.

Aviva and Noam dream that the fish is free from the shark
Gilad sits with Tuval under the shade of the Giving Tree
– in Independence Park
And share a can of beans

---

1 *Gilad Shalit was captured by Hamas militants and held hostage for over five years until his release on October 18, 2011.*

A DAY IN TZFAT

A shekel falls onto the floor. Another shekel. Another shekel. *You snored all night. Now this racket*, Mordechai frowns. *Unintentional*, I say, and leave the room.

I walk down the winding profoundly ancient road to the steps. There, a box rests on a stone, the box painted blue with red letters, "Tzedakah," is charity. I put in two shekels, walk down 100 steps along the ancient graveyard beneath the mountain wearing its green gown. From that mountain's camel hump smoke rises from the bonfire to announce Rosh Chodesh.

At the end of 100 steps, into the icy spring, I immerse. Morning, the Ari Mikvah, when Ari slept, and his soul ascended to heaven to study Torah with tzaddiks. I walk dripping back up the spiraling path to the cobblestone alleyways.

My Aussie friend with a greying beard, dressed in black, dances in the street. I am sure it is for HaShem. He hands me his card. "If I see a need, I consider myself elected."

I follow two bearded men walking into a shul. Rabbi Big Mo is leading Torah study. He teaches me what he knows of the soul at Ascent. His feet are on the ground and his hands reach upwards.

I feel love seeing the pile of rocks – all that is left from the original Abuhav Shul. Rabbi Abuhav flew with the shul from Spain to Tzfat centuries ago; a response to the Spanish inquisition threatening to convert the shul into a church, if only to be destroyed by an earthquake in the 1890s.

Rebeka and I make sandwiches for school children. I put olive oil on the pita and Rebeka sprinkles the zatar. We hear the missile siren. Some call it the Davika or Magic Carpet. When it sounds people say the Meshach is coming.

As butterflies flutter and ascend, around the world we sing Lecha Dodi to welcome the Shabbat Queen. Here – as the people prayed – hundreds of black hens turned white to avoid a governor's decree.

A man sits by me on the rough bench. He arrived here from Alaska ten years ago. We watch the sunset ignite the mountain. He tells me:

People here are building new worlds. There are no traffic lights or McDonald's here. My newly married friends are building a shul in their home. The city understands the chatter of birds and the wind talking to the trees.

I return to my room, find a note from my roommate by a brown pencil case:

Sorry about this morning. This is a gift for your coins. Mordechai

"SHE SAYS SHE LOVES YOU"

The Big Man and I plod slowly through the bustle
of the Arab Quarter. He wears a black kippah.
I wear my green Eagles cap.

A yeshiva student gives out water and Shabbat wine
to us with worn out soles.
The Big Man gulps two cups of Manischewitz.

We walk to the Damascus Gate
and find a bench to rest.

People are bustling this way and that.

The Big Man sings a repertoire of songs.
He belts out, *"She Says She Loves You, Yeah, Yeah, Yeah."*

Last year I heard bullets here.

JOG THROUGH JAFFA GATE

Kiss my fingers (right hand).
Reach out, touch the mezuzah.
Seven steps straight, seven steps left.
L-shaped entry to prevent ancient enemies from invading.
I jog through Jaffa Gate.

By the parking lot of four synagogues
and Diaspora Yeshiva, I see the City of David.

I run down a steep hill to the entrance of the Kotel
and reach in a wooden box for a cardboard kippah.

An old man dressed in white grins.
He remembers me.

GORDON BEACH WEDDING

A sunny veil,
magic between winter storms

Priya from Iowa
Brad from Delaware

The Madras girl and Jerusalem boy
Hum to the seagulls on their wedding day

Chuck and Kris traveled to Mother Teresa's orphanage
To bring their new daughter to Marshalltown

Priya, eight years old and thirty-seven pounds
Now a stubborn angel in her $19.50 wedding gown

Brad saw Priya swimming in the sea
and dreamed of two dolphins dancing

Rabbi Yossi sings seven blessings
A blue-and-white prayer shawl draped over their shoulders

By the churning Mediterranean waves

TEA

Down more than one hundred steps
by an old graveyard and a green mountain
resembling camel humps.

A white towel hangs on a hook.

Water drips into a small pool of water
sunken in a cave. A tzaddik is buried
here. Legend says those that immerse
become pure.

Bobbing in chilly water:
Ad-dah-mah, mah-yeem, shah-mah-yeem.
Earth, water, sky.

I dress without drying off.

In my journal, I write:

My father and I are here together.
Afterwards we walk on the ancient streets of Tzfat
talking and laughing.
My mother joins us for tea.

RED SEA DIVERS

She places a scuba mask over her black abiah.
The instructor puts a scuba hood over his black kipah.

She makes a circle with her thumb and forefinger:
Everything ok.

He signals back:
Everything ok.

They go under,
bubbles rising.

FINDING PEACE OF MIND

"Kadeema, kadeema, Jabul" (Let's go, let's go, Jabul)
"What are you looking for?" grunts Jabul, the camel.

"I'm looking for Peace of Mind.
Do you know where I can find it?"

"What do you think?" growls Jabul.

"I think Peace of Mind is in Tel Aviv
along the Mediterranean Sea.
I can swim and watch the sunset there."

"No, no," says Jabul.
"There is too much traffic and people honking horns.
Try again."

"Is it Jerusalem? People pray there and that is where the
Wailing Wall, Church of the Holy Sepulchre, and the Dome of
the Rock are. It is a magic city of prayer."

"No, no," said Jabul.
"In Jerusalem, Tourist yell at the taxi driver and the taxi
driver yells at his children. Try one more time."

"Then it must be the city of Eilat?"

"No, no!" exclaims Jabul.
"In Eilat, there are far too many loud parties and big hotels."

Jabul turned to the Desert Mountains and points his front
hoof towards there. "That is where you can find Peace of
Mind," says Jabul.
"The stars and the sand are quiet."

CHAVAL AL HA ZMAN: "THE BEST"

Chaval Al Ha Zman: To the soldiers

We are the first volunteers on Hativa 188. There are sixteen of us from Ukraine, Brazil, Holland, South Africa, and the USA. Our base is in the Golan Heights near the Syrian border.

In the War of 1967, eleven tanks from this base halted the advance of five hundred Syrian tanks.

I raised the flag with a soldier today. He had a baby face. I wonder what it must have been like to be here in 67.

Chaval Al Ha Zman: To my roommates

Neil and Ray are my roommates again. They remind me of the Scarecrow and Lion in The Wizard of Oz. When Dorothy lands home from Oz, the Scarecrow and Lion (as her Kansas friends) give Dorothy a happy "You are here!" smile.

Instead of following the Yellow Brick Road to Oz, the three of us land at a different army base every summer. Even though I snore, Neil and Ray put up with me. Neil yells at me for leaving a Coke can on the floor. The Coke draws one thousand ants. Oy vey, not again.

Chaval Al Ha Zman: To the volunteers

Tzvika tells the volunteers that we are part of the base family. So much so, he says that he will check up on us at each of our homes abroad. He is the disciplinary officer at the base and barks out the commands: *Yemina* (right), *Smolla* (left), *Yemina, Smolla.*

The volunteers march. It is my first experience marching. I see a group of soldiers clapp. A volunteer salutes Tzika. She intends to say, *"Ken Mefaked,"* but blurts out, *"Ken Mefager."*

Tzeka turns and says, "She called me a moron." Everybody laughs.

Chaval Al Ha Zman: To the Shayrutim team

Vitaliy says the *Shayrutim* team is the "best of the best." Our team paints the girl's *shayrutim*, or bathroom, better than even Mr. Clean and the White Tornado.

We work hard but have time to tease. Roxy calls Pam, "Wide Zone." I look up and laugh. Later Roxy's explanation is that both of Pam's side pockets have two water bottles each.

Vitaliy puts his hand down the drain without gloves to clean it. He is like "Robot Man" – he never stops working.

Pam loves this job – when she sees the girl soldiers they remind her of her own daughter, who passed away last year.

A soldier walks in and says, "Why do people come from so far to do this – it is unbelievable."

GENIE CAN YOU AND SHE KNOWS

To Tzfat and the Ari mikvah – 1st day – Yom Rishon

Towels wave at me from the clothesline.
I follow a man in black with long paos.
Cubbyholes are hollowed out in the stone wall
I take off my clothes and stuff them there.
Dip my toes into icy spring water and then plunge in.
The cold takes my breath. I bob up and down five times.
Earth, water, sky. Connection.

To the Wailing Wall – 2nd day – Yom Sheni

Bearded men dressed in black
recall Prague two hundred years ago.
I stand next to a man wearing shorts
and a Phillies baseball cap.

They pray. One man sings, *tefillin, tefillin, tefillin.*
I sing *Phillies, Phillies, Phillies.*
He says the words of a prayer. I repeat.
He tells me to close my eyes and visualize those close to me.
I picture Priya, my mother, and Olice
sprinkling water on purple cactus flowers.

To the Red Sea – 3rd day – Yom Shlishi

Reaching out with my right hand (stroke),
with my left hand (stroke),
I swim behind Genie. She rows a boat.
Underneath are Picasso fish, clown fish,
and a mushroom coral. I am a fish too.

Bare brown mountains slip into the blue water.
I part the sea with my hands
and dream of drinking Coke and eating popcorn.

ZAUDY

"The sound comes from your throat, chet, chet," Zaudy
tells me. I try but it is difficult for a native English speaker to
pronounce. Once more, Zaudy encourages me. Zaudy is nineteen
and doing her army service. I am a volunteer for Israel and we
work together testing batteries. Zaudy has become my Hebrew
teacher. Work together for nine weeks in the summer of 2001,
she tells me the story of her journey.

Once each year, white storks fly over Ethiopia
and migrate to Israel.

A Hasida flies over my village
Grandfather and I always sing to her,
"Big white bird,
What is happening in Jerusalem?
Does Jerusalem remember us?"

I am Zaudy. I am eleven years old.
My family lives in a hut shaped in a circle.
It is made from tree branches and mud.

My father is a tanguay, a healer.
My mother is a potter.
We own cows and sheep.
My brother and I take them to water.

Children from the nearby village
taunt us with names and throw stones.
Some people call us falasha: strangers in this land.
They say we change to hyenas at night.
We call ourselves Beta Israel: House of Israel.

On Shabbat, I relax under the Warka trees.
Grandfather tells me stories about Jerusalem.

In Jerusalem he says even the evil ones
turn righteous.

My grandfather recites the name of his father, Berhanu,
his grandfather, Mahari,
his grandfather's father, Kassahun,
his great grandfather's father, Samuel,
his great-great grandfather's father, Desta.

Fifty days after Yom Kippur is the Sigd.
Before the new moon, the Qes, a priest in a white shamma,
climbs the mountain closest to our village.
He is followed by his helper carrying
the Orit (the Torah written in Ge'ez).
Behind follow priests and elders.

They hike up the mountain
like Moses ascended Mount Sinai.
The priest reads from the Orit
in the hope of coming home.

Grandfather makes a deal with G-d –
let him go to see Jerusalem
and die the next day.
The elders march down the mountain
banging drums and playing tin horns.

Father wakes me when the moon is young.
He says we were going back home.
We meet twenty-six others under the Star of David,
mounted on the tin roof of the prayer house.
I walk under the moonlight.

I carry a kamis (dress), netala (shawl),
roasted hummus beans, dust from my home
in a white cloth sack tied to a stick.
Two donkeys carry the water, flour,

chickpeas, onions, spices.
I climb high up steep twisting paths.
Gray and black rocks rise up sharply to the sky.

During the day, we shelter in trees
to hide from robbers and the sun.
I see hyenas, poisonous snakes, lions,
and hear monkeys and frogs.
I hike in the desert that looks
like craters on the moon.

We search for desert ponds,
dig in wet dirt to find water.
Father gives me butter so I can taste the moisture.
Sometimes he chews the bread
and gives it to me so I can swallow it.

On Yom Shishi, Friday, we walk
until the sun is high.
When the moon appears,
we eat special bread and say prayers.
G-d is in the mountain, in the river, in the desert, in the stars.
G-d's instructions are to rest on Shabbat.

After the third star, we begin walking.
I walk for sixteen straight hours.
Grandfather falls asleep on his feet and falls over.
My father says Grandfather has the same destiny as Moses.
I see Moses and Grandfather
by the Star of David on the tin roof.

On the second full moon, we make it to Sudan.
Mother says, "Do not to tell anyone we are Jewish."
If I do, we may die.
Sometimes I have to pray as a Christian,
but in my heart I pray as a Jew.

Sudan is dirty and there is not enough food.
Men take my father away.
He comes back with bandages and broken fingers.
We stay for nine months.
We put sand on all my uncle's children.

Father wakes me under many stars.
A big truck takes us several hours to the airplane.
The airplane is in the shape of a big bird.
Inside I cannot see the front or back.
There are many people.

I hear great noise like thunder.
The airplane rises up in the clouds
like the wings of the big white bird.
I wonder if Jerusalem is in the clouds.
How can something so large stay up in the air?
The plane shakes.
I am afraid to stand up to go to the toilet.
I rest my head on Father.

The airplane lands on the ground.
Father cries out, "Shalom, Shalom, Shalom."
I dream of the bird and talk to Grandfather.

"I cannot believe people are white.
The people talk and sound like birds.
They cannot be human."

Hasida flies over my head.
"Grandfather. We are in Jerusalem."

Around 4,000 of the 15,000 people who started this journey died. They walked 500 kilometers (300 miles). The airlift from Sudan to Israel was made in secret, and called Operation Moses.

When I say goodbye to Zaudy, she waves to me until I am out of sight.

KIBBUTZ

Standing on a wooden bridge,
Lorraine and I look below at the clear
running stream. Two turtles pass each other.
We are volunteers on Kibbutz Maabarot.

Moty, Oystein, and I pile
fifty pound bags of cow feed eight high
and nine in a row. Sometimes they come
tumbling down. We hit the red button
to stop the conveyor belt, but kibbutzniks
hit the green button and more bags rumble toward us.
We, the three stooges, pile them back up.

After work, we crawl under the fence.
One Norwegian, one Russian, and an American
go for a dip in the neighboring kibbutz's swimming pool.

Suzy, a volunteer from Australia, comes later,
and plays Jaws. She tips me off my raft and says,
"Hey mate, how about a bit of choco."
She is after my hidden chocolate supply.

At the end of the summer, I try to leave quietly,
but Lorraine asks me to say goodbye to everyone.
My eyes are a waterfall. My friend gives
me a note to open on the plane.
See you and not goodbye, it says.

In the water, two turtles pass
and go in opposite directions.

SINAI

At the taxi stand I am surrounded

What is the meaning of
these rocks

by Egyptian men who wear traditional
head dresses and gowns. I look out

Do they have wisdom

at the deep blue color of the sea
against the thirsty brown mountains.

What are they
trying to tell me

Three Bedouin children
pose near 6000-year-old   *Sound of silence*
stone huts. The entrances
face the setting sun.
They are tombs.
The soul follows   *Feel the wind*
the setting sun.   *against my face*
                                           My thoughts are empty

Two Bedouin boys look
at me. They are angry.   *The mountains*

The girl looks away.   *are they looking back*

HUMMUS SHOP

"Tear a small piece of pita,
use forefinger and thumb,
dip into hummus, and fold in half,"
Ra'ed instructs me
at the same hummus shop
his father took him as a little boy.

A bearded man wearing a black suit
and kippah walks a mountain bike
past three women with white head scarves
and long black abayas.

Tonight I fly back to the States,
but now I smell the hummus
topped with spiced meat and chickpeas.
We share a large bottle of orange Fanta.

Six of us sit around the table. Tsipi and I
are Jewish. Ra'ed, Mysum, and the others
are Palestinians. All around me
I hear Arabic.

I raise my eyes to look at Ra'ed.
I think,
"You invited me to your favorite hummus shop.
You taught me *marhaba* means hi
and *shokran* is thank you."
Mysum says, "We love you, Brad."

I tell myself to be friends
but in the back of my mind
are cobwebs that are very old.

NO BORDERS (II)

We walk along the beach.
Brown thirsty mountains on one side,
the sparkling clear Red Sea on the other.

I spot a seashell
with imprints of light and dark mountains.

Dafna says to let it be.

This is the same desert that Israel gave
back to Egypt in 1982.

Nature has no borders.

BROWNIES

Dinner is a big salad with fresh tuna, boiled potatoes, `
eggs, tomatoes, cucumbers, string beans, romaine lettuce,
black olives, olive oil and lemon juice.

Shulla and Avraham give me a box of homemade brownies
to take back to the base. They make a deal with me.

"We will not be polite with you and
you will not be polite with us."

Welcome to Israel.

ACKNOWLEDGMENTS AND NOTES

The people I met are like a dream and I want to be together

*Before too long we will part but each of you will be
in my heart forever* – Sinai

I would like to thank these people –

- Priya, my partner in life
- Dr. Carol Gilles for publishing my poems on her office door
- Irwin Kaye for always having an open ear
- Dr. Teresa and Dr. Jennifer for always being there
- Dr. Scott Cairns and Dr. Aliki Barnstone
- Mel Berwin, Berwins, David Doo Doo Berry, Pamela, Efrat, Tsipi, Ester, Moishe
- Dr. Amy Lanin and Dr. Roy Fox – MU Writing Project
- Alice Reese
- Joe Polocco
- Susan Malone
- The Models, Eric Jacobson, Steve Jacobson
- Dr. Melissa Range who would sit with me at the coffee shop working on my poems for several semesters.
- Rabbi Aaron Dyan. He believed in me when I needed a friend.
- Shabtay who was my madrich 20 years ago, but never stopped being my madrich.
- Ray and Neal who were my roommates so many times in SAR-EL.
- The many volunteers and scuba mates from whom I learned so much.

Thanks to the editors of the following publications in which these poems have appeared, sometimes in slightly different versions.

American Development and Internationalization News (University of Missouri): "A Prayer" and parts of "Dreaming of Peace, Taking Notes (II)"

The Jewish Writing Project: "Come In, Come In," "Hummus Shop," "Oasis," "Sammy's Store," and "Lion of Hope"

Poetica: "Sinai", "Sivan, Alone", "Yom Kippur", "Shabbat Shalom"

Sar-El: The National Project for Volunteers for Israel: "Chaval Al Ha Zman," "Upstairs/Downstairs 1947"

Tikkun: "Dreaming of Peace, Taking Notes (I)," "A Prayer"

Voices Israel: "Beggar Woman," "Six Camels," "Falling Star," "A Hasidic Jew and Scuba Diver," "Rooftop in the Old City," "Zaudy," "Red Sea Dive," "Yaacov"

Note that the last stanza from "Yom Kippur" is taken from *Stargirl* by Jerry Spinelli.

I heard an alternate version of "Finding Peace of Mind" on a six-day camel trip in the Negev.

Made in the USA
Monee, IL
13 June 2020